NAKED JUSTICE

John Mortimer
NAKED JUSTICE

OBERON BOOKS
LONDON

First published in 2002 by Oberon Books Ltd.
(incorporating Absolute Classics)
521 Caledonian Road, London N7 9RH
Tel: 020 7607 3637 / Fax: 020 7607 3629

e-mail: oberon.books@btinternet.com

A catalogue record for this book is available from the British
Library.

ISBN: 1 84002 221 3

Cover design: Tim Everett

Cover photograph: John Timbers

Printed in Great Britain by Antony Rowe Ltd, Reading.

In the burrows of the nightmare
Where justice naked is
Time watches from the shadows
And coughs when you would kiss.

W H Auden

Characters

BYRON JOHNSON
aged seventeen

FRED

HUBERT

ELSPETH

KEITH

CASSANDRA CRESSWELL

MR SWIVER

MARSTON DAWLISH, QC

RODDY BOYES

DETECTIVE INSPECTOR DACRE

MR BREADWELL

A town in the North

The present

The stage should be as empty as possible, a table and chairs
being moved for the different locations

Naked Justice was first performed at the Quarry Theatre, West Yorkshire Playhouse, on 26 January 2001, with the following cast:

FRED, Leslie Phillips
KEITH, Nicholas Jones
ELSPETH, Anna Carteret
RODDY BOYES, Rupert Frazer
BYRON, Jimmy Akingbola
HUBERT, Paul Kemp
CASSANDRA, Geraldine Alexander
SWIVER, Gordon Kane
MARSTON DAWLISH, Rupert Baker
DI DACRE, Mark Spalding
BREADWELL, Robin Bowerman

Director, Christopher Morahan
Designer, Simon Higlett

It was subsequently rewritten, and first performed in the new version, as published here, at Birmingham Repertory Theatre, on 12 February 2002, with the following cast:

FRED, Leslie Phillips
KEITH, Simon Ward
ELSPETH, Joanna van Gyseghem
RODDY BOYES, Patrick Ryecart
BYRON, Jimmy Akingbola
HUBERT, Paul Kemp
CASSANDRA, Carolyn Backhouse
SWIVER, Kenneth Jay
MARSTON DAWLISH, Rowland Davies
DI DACRE, Paul Stewart
BREADWELL, Andrew Bolton

Director, Robert Chetwyn
Designer, Hugh Durrant

ACT ONE

Darkness. Suddenly split by the flashing blue lamp of a police car and a wailing siren. In a spotlight, a seventeen-year-old black boy, BYRON JOHNSON, is glimpsed for a moment, then has a mackintosh thrown over his head by a POLICE OFFICER. As they disappear into the shadows, the lights change and we are in:

The living room of a comfortable Victorian town house in a North Country town. There are well-used chairs and a sofa. A writing table with a telephone on it. A television set with its back towards us. HUBERT, around thirty, wearing a white jacket, not altogether clean, and dark trousers, opens a door to let in FRED, grey-haired, wearing a dark suit, untidy, sometimes appearing vague but capable of perception and charm.

FRED: Keith not here yet?

HUBERT: Mr Justice Craxton, as he likes to be known?

FRED: As he very much likes to be known.

HUBERT: There's no sign of him at the moment.

FRED: You'll be making the usual adjustments to Keith's bathroom?

HUBERT: I'm all prepared (*He grins.*) to screw.

FRED: Try not to laugh when you say that, Hubert. Keith was born in desperate need of a humour transplant. Put him in the same room as a joke, it brings him out in a rash. And Miss Justice… No, that sounds ridiculous. I always call her Elspeth.

HUBERT: Our Lady Judge? She arrived early and went straight upstairs. She said she needed a hot bath.

FRED: She says she needs plenty of hot baths. In her line of business.

(*Pause.*)

HUBERT: You here for the big one…?

FRED: What?

HUBERT: Our murder. You going to try that?

FRED: I hardly think so…

HUBERT: I'd've thought they'd given you the big job.

9

FRED: I'd imagine Keith's doing that. In the present circumstances… I think it's the one for Keith.
(*He feels his back. Winces with pain. Sits in an armchair.*)

HUBERT: (*Looks at him silently, then says.*) Can I get you something?

FRED: Yes. You can get me something, Hubert. A whisky. A dark one. The colour of dead bracken, not pale piss. You'll remember how I like it.

HUBERT: I remember.
(*HUBERT goes to the drinks table, looks among the bottles, picks them up, looks at them with increasing frustration while making conversation with FRED.*)
How long since you were last here?

FRED: Last year? It seems like yesterday.

HUBERT: The freezer job, wasn't it?

FRED: I always had my doubts about that freezer business.
(*Pause.*) Freezers play merry hell with the time of death.

HUBERT: Oh, sugar!

FRED: What's the problem?

HUBERT: Silly me. I forgot the whisky. There's something here though.

FRED: What?

HUBERT: Mr Justice Everglades left it. How about a lovely drop of *crème de menthe*?

FRED: 'Totty' Everglades. No doubt he took it *frappé*.

HUBERT: Is that how you like it…?

FRED: Do I look like the ageing hostess of a dubious nightclub?

HUBERT: Not really. Judge Goodwin has bequeathed us. Cherry brandy!

FRED: I thought better of old Goodwin.

HUBERT: Tell you what. Why not try a nice sweet vermouth and soda?

FRED: (*Uncertain.*) Do I have to?

HUBERT: (*Pouring vermouth and soda.*) Lovely drink. You'll look really trendy with a glass of that in your hand. 'Fly me to glamorous Yorkshire on the wings of a sweet vermouth!'
(*He hands the drink to FRED, who winces as he moves to take it.*)
(*Sympathetic.*) No better, is it…?

FRED: Our job. Buggers up the back. Over the course of years.

HUBERT: I told you! You need my cosmic pedal digital manipulation. It exercises your toes and gets you in touch with the universe.

FRED: Hubert. You've got no medical qualifications whatsoever.

HUBERT: (*Hurt.*) I used to go out with a masseuse. He taught me all I know.

FRED: (*Drinking.*) Fairly short relationship, was it?

HUBERT: I wish you'd try not to be sarcastic. Your weakness, isn't it? Being sarky.

FRED: Probably.

HUBERT: Anyway. I just want you to relax.

FRED: When people say 'relax!', I always go quite stiff with anxiety.

(*Pause. HUBERT looks at him.*)

HUBERT: Enjoying our sweet vermouth are we?

FRED: (*Takes another drink, makes a face.*) Not much.
(*At HUBERT's look of disappointment.*) Oh, all right. *Quite* enjoying it. What time's dinner?

HUBERT: Seven-thirty, as per. Provided Mr Justice Craxton's train's on time. Tonight, I'm very much afraid, Mother's doing you a paella. She watches those cooking programmes. 'A taste of the Mediterranean sun.' It's been her downfall.

(*ELSPETH enters, attractive, forties, energetic.*)

FRED: Welcome, Elspeth. Darling of the Divorce Court. The Madonna of the Family Division.

ELSPETH: (*With affection.*) How are you, Uncle Fred?

FRED: Surviving…

ELSPETH: Keith's not here yet…?

FRED: We're enjoying a period of remission.

(*She moves to the drinks table, inspects it.*)

ELSPETH: What happened to the whisky…?

FRED: Done a runner.

HUBERT: (*Pouring her a drink.*) Have a nice sweet vermouth. You'll enjoy that. *Molto delicioso*, vermouth.

ELSPETH: Who says so?

HUBERT: The telly.

ELSPETH: Is there gin?

HUBERT: (*Looking at the bottles.*) Oh, yes. Plenty of gin.

ELSPETH: And tonic?

(*HUBERT makes the drink.*)

FRED: Had a nice bath, did you?

ELSPETH: Glorious. It's the only place where I can forget
– the horrors of family life. When I'm in court I'm
dreaming of Floribunda's Hollyhock Bath Gel. I imagine
myself sinking into cleansing bubbles.
(*HUBERT hands ELSPETH her drink and goes. ELSPETH
brings her drink and sits near FRED. She drinks.*)
Sometimes I wonder how I got landed with this job.
I was a model child in so many ways. Helpful. Polite to
my parents. Looked after the young ones. Head of
school. Voted the girl most likely to.

FRED: Most likely to what?

ELSPETH: Hardly ever masturbated... Worked hard to get
where I am.

FRED: Where you are? Exactly!

ELSPETH: The case I'm starting tomorrow. It hardly bears
thinking about this husband!

FRED: Tell me about him.

ELSPETH: If you're really interested...

FRED: It passes the time, while we're waiting for Keith.

ELSPETH: I don't know how people find out they like such
things.

FRED: What sort of things?

ELSPETH: (*With disgust.*) Chocolate cakes.

FRED: He had a sweet tooth?

ELSPETH: Nothing like that. He enjoyed sitting on them.
And he wanted his wife to sit on them too. If you had the
slightest affection for me, he used to say, you'd join the
splodgers.

FRED: What are they? Football supporters?

ELSPETH: Don't you believe it. People who get erotic
delight from sitting on food.

FRED: (*Looking at the paper.*) Absolutely nothing on telly tonight.

ELSPETH: I mean, how did he discover that was what he wanted to do?

FRED: *A Call Girl Remembers.*

ELSPETH: (*Frowns.*) Is that how he found out?

FRED: No. It's a programme on Channel Four.

ELSPETH: Do you think he was born knowing it? Or did it come to him in a blinding flash one day?

FRED: On an early birthday. Perhaps his mother made him a cake.

ELSPETH: Chocolate...

FRED: With candles. And 'Happy Birthday' written in icing. And he said, 'I say, Mum. What a super cake. Would you mind if I sat on it a moment?' (*He looks at the paper again.*) *The Wonders of Nature.* 'A stunning documentary on the life cycle of the prawn.'

ELSPETH: I meant to ask you... A friend of mine...

FRED: Unusual to have a friend. In our particular line of business.

ELSPETH: I thought I might ask him to dinner. On Thursday.

FRED: Here?

ELSPETH: Yes. Here. Can you see any objection...?

FRED: Only... Well, I suppose I want to keep you to myself. You invite your...

ELSPETH: Friend.

FRED: Boy friend?

ELSPETH: Well... Perhaps.

FRED: Exactly! And you'll be off whispering in corners. And I'll be left to hear how brilliantly Keith got a hundred per cent conviction in the Croydon Savings Bank job.

ELSPETH: Uncle Fred... You know I love going on circuit with you. But...

FRED: But what?

ELSPETH: Well, Keith won't want us to have guests.

FRED: That's true. (*Thinks it over.*) Then let's invite him. If it'll annoy Keith.

ELSPETH: He's quite fun.

FRED: You can't be talking about Keith?

ELSPETH: My friend. His name's Roddy Boyes.

FRED: I won't hold that against him.

ELSPETH: Lives round here. Keeps a lot of horses. He's rather an amusing chartered accountant.

FRED: Isn't that an oxymoron? You know, like hot ice... Or the wit and wisdom of Keith.

(*KEITH enters with a strangely-shaped parcel wrapped in plastic, and a briefcase. He is in his forties, upright, unsmiling, an alarmingly serious Judge who sticks to the letter of the law.*)

Oh, hullo, Keith. I see you've brought your lavatory seat with you.

KEITH: (*Calls.*) Hubert...

(*HUBERT enters. KEITH gives him the parcel, which he fits under one arm.*)

For my bathroom.

HUBERT: Right! My screwdriver's at the ready.

(*HUBERT goes.*)

ELSPETH: Good evening, Keith.

KEITH: How are you, Elspeth?

FRED: Clean. She's amazingly clean.

KEITH: So. We're all here.

FRED: Apparently...

KEITH: A load of heavy work ahead.

FRED: And absolutely nothing on telly. I have to say, I do miss *Blind Date*.

KEITH: I rather think we'll all have work to do in the evenings.

FRED: What I could never understand about *Blind Date* was the way they never seemed to get down to rogering.

KEITH: I have very little idea...what you're talking about.

FRED: They got so easily put off. 'I wasn't at all impressed by the way he slurped his soup during our first candle-lit dinner in the gourmet restaurant.' I mean, they'd gone off to Jersey to roger each other, not to fuss about their table manners. That's the way I look at it.

(*Pause.*)

KEITH: There is one thing, though, I'd like to make absolutely crystal clear at the outset.

FRED: Blind dates seem to be a complete turn-off, so far as rogering is concerned.

ELSPETH: (*Gloomily.*) Unlike chocolate cake.

KEITH: I can only hope, in the course of time, your conversation may become intelligible to me. Meanwhile, there's one thing I must emphasise.

FRED: Go on, old sport. Emphasise it.

KEITH: The clear understanding was that, of the two available bathrooms, you and Elspeth should share one. And I'd have the one nearest my bedroom door...for my sole use.

FRED: In solitary splendour.

KEITH: Those were the clear terms of our agreement. I took it to be binding on you both.

FRED: You mean we can't just pop into your loo. In case of emergency?

(*KEITH looks appalled.*)

Don't worry, old sport. Only joking.

(*He gets up, moves to the drinks table.*)

Do you want a drink? I'm afraid there's no whisky.

(*HUBERT enters, speaks to ELSPETH.*)

HUBERT: There's a gentleman on the 'phone for you...

ELSPETH: Thank you, Hubert. (*She goes.*)

KEITH: What happened to the whisky?

FRED: Hubert had a lapse of memory.

KEITH: Typical! Can I have a glass of mineral water?

FRED: I suppose you can. Although I don't see a whole lot of point in mineral water. (*Pours water, takes it to KEITH.*)

KEITH: (*Drinks mineral water, then says.*) Aren't you a little worried about Hubert?

FRED: I worry about practically everything. Except Hubert. You mean his mother's cooking? Normal things, like toad-in-the-hole and rice pudding, are a closed book to Hubert's Mum.

KEITH: Do you think it's entirely safe, having him in this job?

FRED: You're afraid he might make a pass? Elspeth and I are here to protect you.

KEITH: (*Sighing.*) Fred. Do you think you could take *something* seriously?

FRED: Oh, I do. Lots of things. Toad-in-the-hole. And rice pudding.

KEITH: Doesn't it occur to you that people of Hubert's sexual orientation tend to be indiscreet? They gossip, you know. They tell tales. They haunt doubtful clubs and spread scandalous stories...

FRED: If anyone has a scandalous story to spread about me, I think I'd find it immensely flattering.

KEITH: (*Not listening.*) His work here... He may know a little too much about us.

FRED: You're afraid news of your lavatory seat may leak... To the *Yorkshire Post*? So far as I can make out, Hubert regards our lives as something of a joke.

KEITH: That's what I'm afraid of.

FRED: You're afraid of jokes?

(*KEITH stares at him, doesn't answer.*)

FRED: As far as his sexual orientation goes... I can only hope he enjoys it. No doubt it makes a pleasant contrast to life with Mother.

KEITH: I remain...uneasy about Hubert.

(*Pause.*)

FRED: It's not Hubert I'm worried about. I can't help thinking about them.

KEITH: Who?

FRED: All the people who've been waiting for us. (*Pause.*) And now we're here.

(*Light change. Light fades on the room. Pool of light downstage, where CASSANDRA CRESSWELL, serious and hard-working, is seated looking through a bundle of papers. SWIVER, older, more relaxed and less senior, is standing, also looking down at the papers. They are both dressed in dark, formal clothes.*)

CASSANDRA: (*Reading.*) Blood on the sleeve of the fleece he put out for his mother to wash.

SWIVER: His birth mother.

CASSANDRA: Yes. His birth mother. Placidity Johnson.

SWIVER: She runs 'Bammy's'. Caribbean cuisine. Quite interesting. You ever eaten there, have you?

CASSANDRA: Blood of the victim's group.

SWIVER: Afraid so. Baked black crabs, they do at 'Bammy's'. Don't you ever eat Caribbean?

CASSANDRA: Three wounds. Not inconsistent with a kitchen knife. And they never found the weapon...

SWIVER: I'd put you down as Thai. Am I right? You tried 'The Midnight Garden'? It's in that new shopping mall. Opposite the bus station.

CASSANDRA: Full confession.

SWIVER: Of course. Isn't there always? (*Pause.*) I don't mean 'The King of Bangkok', down by the multi-storey.

CASSANDRA: Signed. (*She puts the papers in a briefcase.*) He didn't make things easy for us.

SWIVER: Do they ever? Stewed cat and bean shoots. That's what they serve you down 'The King of Bangkok'. Have we got a run?

CASSANDRA: What do you think...?

SWIVER: I think... Worry about it when we see him.
(*They cross the stage to where, over in another pool of light, we see BYRON JOHNSON, a seventeen-year-old boy, is sitting at a table. Born in the town, he speaks with a North Country accent. SWIVER also sits. CASSANDRA stands, asking questions.*)

BYRON: Started when Winston...

CASSANDRA: Winston Jardine?

BYRON: Him. He move in the Bammy Restaurant. Move in with my birth mother.

CASSANDRA: With Placidity...?

BYRON: And Placidity bring him tea in bed, wash out his clothes, give money to him and he's cheating on her the whole time! Sometimes in the place he keep down Jubilee Road where he does dealing and all of that. Sometimes he don't even bother to move out of the restaurant...

CASSANDRA: I take it you and Winston didn't get on, exactly.

BYRON: He always laugh at me. Calls me ignorant. Thick head! Numbskull. You know what that word means?

CASSANDRA: I've got an idea.

BYRON: I no more ignorant than what he is. What he did with Fleur.

CASSANDRA: Your sister…?

BYRON: She didn't want to do it. She's too young and she didn't want it. Started when Placidity in the hospital. Winston Jardine made her do it.

CASSANDRA: And so…?

BYRON: So there is why I called on him. Down Jubilee Road. Told him to stop it with Fleur.

CASSANDRA: What did he say?

BYRON: Nothing. He say nothing. He's dead when I got there. (*Grins.*) Too dead to say anything at all!
(*Pause.*)

CASSANDRA: You say the door was open?

BYRON: Open. Somebody knife him. Not before it was time to do so.

CASSANDRA: Did you read your statement to the police? You signed it.

BYRON: (*Contemptuous.*) 'Course I read it!

CASSANDRA: (*Reading from it.*) 'I stabbed Winston three times. I think I got him in the chest and twice in the stomach. I was in a daze after. I threw away the knife. I can't tell you where. It's a blank what I did after.' Did you tell the police that?

BYRON: No.

CASSANDRA: Not any of it?

BYRON: None of it.

CASSANDRA: (*Giving him the document.*) Read it again. Think about how much of it is true. (*She stands up.*) We'll be back.

SWIVER: We'll be back.

(*Light fades on BYRON. CASSANDRA and SWIVER move away from him to downstage centre.*)

CASSANDRA: What do you think now?

SWIVER: I think… We keep the worst news from him.

CASSANDRA: Which is?

SWIVER: (*Gloomy.*) Mr Justice Keith Craxton has come here to try this case.

CASSANDRA: What can we do about that?

SWIVER: (*Brightening up.*) Nothing. What do you say we go Chinese for lunch? They do Peking up by the Leisure Centre.

(*They go.*)

(*Light on the lodgings. ELSPETH and FRED are playing backgammon and drinking whisky.*)

FRED: How's your Matrimonial?

ELSPETH: (*Sighs.*) There've been developments. The wretched husband agreed to go to a psychiatrist.

FRED: For cake sitting?

ELSPETH: It seems she's an expert in the subject. You can see why I don't want to get married.

FRED: (*Looking at her.*) I don't want you to get married either.

ELSPETH: Oh, come on, Fred. I intend to devote myself entirely to no goods. I'm only interested in someone gorgeous who has absolutely no respect for married life.

FRED: Men who'd bolt at the faintest whiff of orange blossom? Is *he* like that?

ELSPETH: Who?

FRED: Your boyfriend. On Thursday.

ELSPETH: Oh. Yes. I'll be pretty safe with him. He's allergic to marriage.

FRED: (*Sits.*) Odd, that. Lucy rather took to it.

ELSPETH: Your wife?

FRED: It was the songs. Brought us together.

ELSPETH: Songs?

FRED: We soon found out. We both knew the words of songs. Not just the choruses, you understand, but the verses. Not many people know those…

ELSPETH: I don't suppose they do…

FRED: Songs don't have words any more.

ELSPETH: You all say that…

FRED: We do?

ELSPETH: People of your age.

FRED: Words! We used to sing them, all over the place. In
cars… Walking in woods. In bed…very often.
(*Sings.*) 'Our romance won't end on a sorrowful note,
Though tomorrow you're gone;
The song is ended, but as the songwriter wrote,
"The melody lingers on."
They may take you from me,
I'll miss your fond caress.
But though they take you from me,
I'll still possess…'
You know what that leads into…?

ELSPETH: No idea.

FRED: (*Sings again.*) 'The way you wear your hat,
The way you sip your tea,
The mem'ry of all that –
No, no! They can't take that away from me!'
(*Pause.*)
She was unfaithful to me, of course.
(*He sits and then sings again.*)
'We may never, never meet again
On the bumpy road to love…'
(*He stops singing.*) She cheated me. With death… (*Pause.*)
'It's a bit of a bugger,' she told me. 'I'm going to die.'
She wrote out all sorts of lists. What to do about the
boiler. Her favourite shops. How to scramble eggs. Lists
of instructions. As though she were going away on
holiday. (*Pause.*) I don't know why I'm telling you all
this… It was a long time ago.

ELSPETH: Yes.

FRED: Last day. Well, I tried all our songs on her. But there
was only one she wanted. Ridiculous! My father used to
sing it, at Christmas.

ELSPETH: What was it? 'The Holly and the Ivy'?
(*FRED sings very loudly – another 1920s song. KEITH enters.
Looks round as though to find something to object to.*)

KEITH: You're drinking whisky!

FRED: (*Drinking.*) You got us. Bang to rights!

KEITH: Hubert remembered? (*He sits.*)

FRED: No. Hubert didn't remember...

KEITH: Then how?

FRED: We went down the offy.

KEITH: (*Incredulous.*) You did *what?*

FRED: Visited the off licence. Corner of Mulberry Road. Between the betting shop and the Adult Interest Videos... Do I have to keep translating for you?

KEITH: (*Goes to the drinks table, pours himself a whisky.*) Am I to understand... You and Elspeth went into an off licence. Together?

ELSPETH: We kept each other company.

KEITH: You went into a *public* off licence?

FRED: It appeared to be open to the public.

KEITH: It didn't occur to you... You might be recognised?

FRED: I don't think so. We didn't hear anyone saying, 'Look, there go Elspeth and Fred buying two bottles of Bell's with a Visa card.' Did you hear anyone say that, Elspeth?

ELSPETH: No one at all.

FRED: Will you take your oath on it?

ELSPETH: I swear... By Almighty God.

KEITH: Were you...*approached?*

FRED: I'm afraid I'm getting a little past the approachable age. Were you approached, Elspeth?

ELSPETH: No one approached me.

KEITH: What would have happened if there had been habitual criminals in the off licence?

FRED: Well, I imagine there were. Don't you, Elspeth?

ELSPETH: Probably.

FRED: There aren't many off licences you can go into these days that haven't got a habitual criminal or two, taking a look at the special offers.

KEITH: They might be people we'll end up having to try...

FRED: Not Elspeth. Unless their marriages are on the rocks. Did any of them say their marriages were on the rocks,

Elspeth, and they were after a bottle of Smirnoff to forget?

ELSPETH: No one spoke to me.

FRED: None of our customers were there, apparently.

KEITH: What are all the people of this town going to think if they see a couple of Her Majesty's Judges wandering around an off licence...buying whatever you said.

FRED: They might possibly think that Judges are human beings like the rest of us. You wouldn't like that, would you, Keith? (*Gets up, pours more drinks.*)

KEITH: You know perfectly well. When we arrive in a town we're meant to keep...a little apart. A little...aloof. We have duties as well as privileges.

FRED: I know. You want to bang us up. In the nick. Sentenced to live together. Away from our homes and loved ones. Those of us who've got any loved ones left. We're not meant to go disco dancing, or slink into Singles Shopping Night at the supermarket. According to you, we've been given a custodial sentence!
(*He hands a drink to KEITH. KEITH drinks, then looks hard, and with hostility, at FRED.*)

KEITH: This is my home town, Fred. If you can all it a home. A space curtained off in Mother's bedsit, behind the station hotel.

FRED: You do tell us that...every time we come here.

KEITH: Mother was a chambermaid...

FRED: We remember.

KEITH: A way of life you've never experienced...

FRED: I have to admit. No such word as 'chambermaid' appears on my CV.

KEITH: You've never seen the underside of life. You've no idea. What was left behind in various bedrooms!

FRED: I can imagine...

KEITH: (*Drinks.*) You can't. They made use of the place. To do things they'd never do at home. And left the mess for decent people to clean up. Like Mother. I'll never forget what she found...on one occasion.

FRED: A severed finger...?

KEITH: No...

ELSPETH: A chocolate cake!

(*ELSPETH and FRED look at each other, suppress laughter.*)

KEITH: (*Suspicious.*) What's the matter with you two?

ELSPETH: Nothing.

FRED: Nothing whatsoever.

(*Pause. He looks at KEITH's glass.*)

You've drunk all the off licence whisky. You'd like another?

(*KEITH shakes his head.*)

KEITH: And another thing... It's completely unacceptable.

FRED: What's unacceptable now?

KEITH: The so-called dinner they served up to us. Our first night here!

FRED: Those rather nervous-looking prawns? Peering out of yellow rice? Not a particularly happy dish.

ELSPETH: Oh, you mean the paella?

KEITH: (*With rising indignation.*) I don't care what it's called. That was disgusting and since then it's got steadily worse. You've got to speak to Wendy about it.

FRED: I have?

KEITH: Of course, Uncle Fred. It's your department. As the...

FRED: Oldest?

ELSPETH: The most...experienced.

KEITH: The Senior Judge. A privileged position.

FRED: Of course. You try the murders. I do the serious stuff. Like ticking off the cook. You know if I did that, Hubert would be terribly upset.

KEITH: Why on earth?

FRED: Well, of course he would. Wendy is his mother.

KEITH: Is that some sort of mitigating circumstance?

FRED: She gets these wretched concoctions off the television. She was proud of it. She thinks she's achieved some sort of culinary miracle.

KEITH: Then you must disillusion her.

FRED: So why don't *you* tell her?

KEITH: Why should I do your job?

FRED: Because you'd probably love it. She'll be terribly hurt...

KEITH: Force yourself, Fred! Have the courage to find somebody guilty for once in your life.

(*Light change. FRED, KEITH and ELSPETH go.*)

(*Light downstage. BYRON and SWIVER are sitting, CASSANDRA is standing.*)

CASSANDRA: When you saw Winston on the floor. What did you do?

BYRON: Don't know what you mean…

SWIVER: Did you, by any chance, kneel down?

BYRON: That's what I did. Kneel down. To see if he's dead, like…

CASSANDRA: Might you have touched him?

BYRON: Might have…

CASSANDRA: I'm thinking about the blood on your sleeve…

BYRON: Sure. I touched him. Yes.

SWIVER: And then?

BYRON: I go home. Back to 'Bammy's'…

SWIVER: You were seen…coming out of Winston's room.

BYRON: I don't remember.

CASSANDRA: Did you tell anyone what you'd found?

BYRON: (*With rising anger.*) Why you ask me these questions?

CASSANDRA: It's my job.

BYRON: Be on my side. Help me. That's your job, isn't it?

CASSANDRA: I can't do my job unless you answer my questions. (*Pause.*) Or at least some of them.

BYRON: (*Angrier.*) Questions! Always questions!

CASSANDRA: The police asked you plenty of questions. In the car when you were arrested…

BYRON: Some… They asked me some…

CASSANDRA: Did they ask you why you went down to see Winston?

BYRON: I think so…

CASSANDRA: You think so? Did you read your statement again?

BYRON: I read it! Of course I read it…

CASSANDRA: Let me remind you. I've got another copy. Just read it again. Out loud.

(*She hands BYRON a copy. He looks at it. Silence.*)

Well…

BYRON: I'm reading it...

CASSANDRA: Aloud, please! Read it aloud...

BYRON: Why?

CASSANDRA: You can do that, can't you?

BYRON: (*Hurt.*) 'Course I can...

CASSANDRA: All right. How does it begin? Just a couple of sentences.

BYRON: (*Hesitant.*) 'I go down to see Winston in Jubilee Road because I didn't like what he's doing to my sister.'

CASSANDRA: (*She takes back the copy.*) It doesn't say that at all...

(*Light change. CASSANDRA and SWIVER go.*)

(*Light on the lodgings. FRED sitting. HUBERT standing.*)

FRED: (*With difficulty.*) Hubert. I've got something quite serious to say to you...

HUBERT: Back still playing up?

FRED: The back is much as always. This is about the dinners.

HUBERT: Mother's anxious about them...

FRED: Is she really?

HUBERT: She keeps on at me. 'Did they enjoy my rice and seafood Mediterranean-style dish the first night?' 'They haven't said,' I tell her, and she looks anxious. It's my belief she's losing sleep over it.

FRED: That's not necessary!

HUBERT: Can I give her a word of reassurance?

(*Pause. FRED makes up his mind.*)

FRED: I don't see why not...

HUBERT: You're telling me...it went down well?

FRED: Remarkably well.

HUBERT: Greatly enjoyed.

FRED: We loved it.

HUBERT: And since then...

FRED: Tell Wendy she's not to worry.

HUBERT: That's going to be a considerable weight off her mind.

FRED: (*Anxious.*) It's not paella tonight, is it? Elspeth's got a guest...

HUBERT: Her boyfriend?

FRED: Her friend.

HUBERT: Cassoulet.

FRED: (*Fearing the worst.*) What's that?

HUBERT: Mother's doing cassoulet. Sausages, cut up and floating around in a sort of brown substance. Provençal cassoulet. She got it off the television. She's pinned a lot of hopes on it.

FRED: Of course. I understand. Thank you, Hubert.

(HUBERT goes. FRED picks up the paper, and quietly sings a well-known 1920s song. KEITH enters.)

KEITH: I saw Hubert.

FRED: So did I.

KEITH: You've had a word with him?

FRED: A word or two.

(Pause.)

KEITH: He didn't look particularly upset.

FRED: Did you want him to be?

KEITH: Naturally. You were going to tell him that Spanish whatever it is, was completely unacceptable…

FRED: Yes. I was…

KEITH: So you made it clear?

FRED: No, I didn't.

KEITH: What?

FRED: I said we loved it.

(Pause.)

KEITH: (*Coldly angry.*) We were relying on you.

FRED: Wendy was proud of that paella. She'd had sleepless nights wondering if we liked it. So what does it matter? I couldn't hurt her feelings.

KEITH: Then, may I say…you're completely unfitted for our line of business.

FRED: I think you've already made that clear…

KEITH: I don't know what you mean.

FRED: Don't you? Didn't you have a word in the right places? A glass of sherry with the Chief Justice? A port with old Tredgold from the Lord Chancellor's office… I know exactly why I was taken off crime.

KEITH: You were taken off crime because you wouldn't make people face the consequences of their evil actions. As in the case of Wendy and her abysmal cooking. (*Pause.*)

FRED: You have to bend the rules from time to time…for the sake of humanity.

KEITH: (*Laughing.*) Bend the rules! You think you're above the rules… Far, far above them! You think it's all right for you – to laugh at the rules?

FRED: It's all right for anyone…

KEITH: Anyone privileged? You were born into this job. It opened its arms to you! And your face fitted.

FRED: Fitted what?

KEITH: The net. The old boys' net. I had to work for my chances. I had to fight every inch of the way… To get where I am…

FRED: And I'm sure it does you enormous credit.

KEITH: You don't sound as though you think it's very fair.

FRED: It's exactly how fair you think it is.

KEITH: Where I came from. In the back streets of this town. In places you've never been to. They've forgotten all the rules… And I'm here to remind them… Forcibly…

FRED: What about trying to understand them… Isn't that…occasionally important…?

KEITH: They need rules! They can't live a decent life without them…

FRED: So if they go commit some outrageous crime – like cooking a dubious paella – they should be sent to prison for life?

KEITH: I suppose you think that's funny? Let me tell you, Fred – you're not nearly as funny as you think you are. (*The men are standing, staring at each other, hostile. ELSPETH enters, carefully made-up, wearing a black cocktail dress, a little jewellery.*)

ELSPETH: Are you two boys quarrelling again?

KEITH: Fred has failed to do his obvious duty.

ELSPETH: Have you, Uncle Fred?

FRED: I feel unusually relaxed. There's nothing like failing to do your duty to give you a little glow of satisfaction.

ELSPETH: So. What's going on?

FRED: We were having a deep, philosophical argument about Wendy's cooking.

KEITH: You know it wasn't just that.

ELSPETH: Please don't quarrel. Either of you. I'm so looking forward to dinner tonight…

KEITH: You shouldn't. Nothing's changed in the kitchen.

FRED: We'll hope for the best. (*To ELSPETH.*) And you're looking exotic.

ELSPETH: Of course. I've got a guest, remember?

KEITH: Are you trying to tell me… You've invited a guest here tonight. To the lodgings.

ELSPETH: Of course.

KEITH: Has this been discussed?

FRED: Certainly. And I made my decision. As the Senior Judge. Remember the rules, Keith. Just try to take them seriously.

(*Pause. KEITH decides to ignore FRED. Speaks to ELSPETH.*)

KEITH: Who is this guest exactly?

FRED: Her young man's coming to dinner.

ELSPETH: Not so young. But a bit devastating.

(*HUBERT enters.*)

HUBERT: The gentleman's here.

(*KEITH, angry at the others for inviting a guest, turns away and starts reading the papers on his desk. He doesn't look up as RODDY enters. He's only a year or two younger than KEITH but he looks much younger. He is handsome with longish hair, wears a blazer with gold buttons and some sort of sporting club tie. FRED advances towards RODDY.*)

FRED: I'm Fred Dotteridge. You must be Roddy.

RODDY: Afraid so. Haven't got much choice. I say, Elspeth. You all look jolly comfortable here.

FRED: Fond of the Spice Girls, are you?

RODDY: They were rather gorgeous.

FRED: A bit out of date, I know. And I hope you think *we're* gorgeous. I'm Posh Spice. At least, I *was*. Elspeth's Baby Spice. Now, let's have a minute's silence. While Keith says, 'What are the Spice Girls?'

(*KEITH says nothing.*)

Keith...is Scary Spice.

(*KEITH turns and now looks at RODDY for the first time.*)

RODDY: (*Holds out his hand to KEITH.*) We've met before...

FRED: How nice.

(*KEITH turns and looks at RODDY, holds out his hand. FRED watches them as the light fades.*)

(*Lights come up downstage. CASSANDRA and MARSTON DAWLISH, ex-public school, superior, large and fat, in his thirties, is patronising her. They are on bar stools at a chromium hotel bar. Muzak is playing.*)

DAWLISH: Poor old Lord Byron.

CASSANDRA: Don't make fun of his name.

DAWLISH: He'll go no more a'roving. At least, not for the next fifteen years or so.

CASSANDRA: Don't you be too sure.

DAWLISH: That's the spirit! It'll be fun prosecuting you.

CASSANDRA: Don't you be too sure of that, either.

(*Pause. DAWLISH looks at her approvingly, then.*)

DAWLISH: I really want to help you.

CASSANDRA: Oh, is *that* what you want?

DAWLISH: We don't have to spend days on this, do we? Advise his Lordship to plead guilty. He'd be out sooner.

CASSANDRA: Because he says he didn't do it.

DAWLISH: He says...? He's already confessed...

CASSANDRA: Why don't you just wait and see...?

DAWLISH: What're you hinting at? Self-defence? Provocation? I might be prepared to consider a plea to manslaughter. Just between friends.

CASSANDRA: Is that what we are? (*She drinks.*) I'm going to fight for an acquittal.

DAWLISH: (*Looking at her.*) Brave.

CASSANDRA: What?

DAWLISH: Something brave and sexy about you. A little bit of crackling in a wig...determined to fight the impossible fight.

CASSANDRA: Has anyone ever told you how totally disgusting you are?

DAWLISH: (*Smiling.*) Heaps of people! They tell me all the time!

29

CASSANDRA: I suppose you find it rather flattering.

DAWLISH: I don't believe it.

CASSANDRA: You don't believe you're totally disgusting?

DAWLISH: I don't believe that if I gave a discreet tap on the door of Number Fifty-One, you wouldn't open up to me.

(*Pause. CASSANDRA looks at him, thinks it over, then.*)

CASSANDRA: Out of the question.

DAWLISH: Why, exactly?

CASSANDRA: Byron wouldn't like it. He's all alone in an airless cell that smells of disinfectant and stale piss and how could he stand the thought of his brief being fucked by the prosecution?

DAWLISH: He'd never know.

CASSANDRA: That doesn't matter.

DAWLISH: (*Grandly.*) A mere client. He's not so important as the great tradition of fellowship of the Bar.

CASSANDRA: The great fellowship of the bar in a Trusthouse on circuit doesn't require me to be fallen on by a hugely overweight Christmas turkey with its front claw stuck out.

DAWLISH: (*Smiling.*) Too bad...

CASSANDRA: Sorry.

DAWLISH: So am I. It means we've got a fight on our hands.

CASSANDRA: To the death.

(*They clink glasses and drink to each other. Light fades on the bar. CASSANDRA and DAWLISH go.*)

(*We see the lodgings, now only lit by a light on the table beside KEITH's papers. HUBERT enters, helping FRED, who is in considerable pain in his back.*)

HUBERT: It's playing up again...?

FRED: No. This time it's completely serious.

HUBERT: Was it Elspeth's boyfriend? Bit of pain in the backside...

FRED: The entertaining accountant.

HUBERT: I couldn't fancy him.

FRED: I don't think you'll be required to. (*Stab of pain.*) Ouch!

HUBERT: It's time you let me try it.

FRED: (*Suspicious.*) Try what, exactly?

HUBERT: Cosmic pedal digital manipulation.

FRED: Hubert... I don't need it.

HUBERT: Let me give it a whirl, girl!

FRED: I've got enough on my plate without having you get me in touch with the universe.

HUBERT: If you'd at least lie down flat, you'd feel the better for it.

FRED: Do you honestly think so?

HUBERT: No harm in trying, is there? If you were flat on your back with your head on the phone books...

FRED: Well...

HUBERT: It can't do any harm.

FRED: I suppose not. All right, then.

HUBERT: There's my Fred!

(*HUBERT puts the phone book down behind the sofa. FRED lowers himself gingerly to the ground, and then lies flat. In this position, FRED is out of sight of the audience or others coming into the room. We see HUBERT's head over the back of the sofa.*)

Let's have your shoes off, Uncle Fred. No. Don't bother. I can work through the sock.

FRED: Oh, well done!

HUBERT: Nice little feet you've got on you. I bet you were a dancer in your younger years! Rhumba, at all, did you? Now, flat on your back. Close your eyes.

FRED: You're tickling

HUBERT: Don't talk. Empty your mind now.

FRED: (*Sleepy.*) No problem.

HUBERT: Think of...blue. Blue shirt. Blue frock.

FRED: Frock or sock?

HUBERT: Whatever you want to think about that's blue. While I gently manoeuvre your toes...

FRED: (*Very sleepy.*) Delightful.

HUBERT: The pain's going out of those toe ends. Through the sock. The pain is draining away. Slowly. Draining away. Keep thinking of blue. Do you mind? Just blue... Lovely. Deep blue. No pain... No pain at all. Now then. Sleep well, Uncle Fred.

(HUBERT gets up and leaves the room quietly after having turned off the reading lamp on the table. The room is in darkness. KEITH enters, not in a good mood. Starts to collect his work – documents – from the table. As he does so, RODDY comes in. He is smoking a cigar.)

RODDY: Good stories.

KEITH: What?

RODDY: Fred has some good stories.

KEITH: Ten.

RODDY: Ten?

KEITH: Ten good stories. He plays them almost every evening. Like the ten favourite tunes he'd take to a desert island.

(Pause.)

RODDY: Pity about his back. Oh, by the way, I liked the one about the judge who said he'd written out his judgement but he'd left it in his cottage in Wales so they'd have to wait for the post...

KEITH: We know...

RODDY: And this helpful barrister said, 'Fax it up, my Lord.' *(Laughing.)* And the judge said, 'Yes, it does rather!'

KEITH: *(Going back to work.)* You don't have to tell me. We know it by heart.

RODDY: I hadn't heard it before.

KEITH: What?

RODDY: *(Louder.)* I said, I rather enjoyed it. I hadn't heard it before.

KEITH: You'll forgive me. I have to work.

RODDY: Of course. Mind if I pour myself a drink?

(He goes to the drinks table, puts down his cigar and looks at the bottles.)

KEITH: There may not be any whisky...

RODDY: I'm easy. *(Pause, then he says louder.)* I said, I'm easily satisfied. *(Pours a drink, looks round.)* Fine old house, this...

KEITH: *(At work.)* Yes.

RODDY: Just kept open...for you lot?

KEITH: Yes. It's reserved for us.

RODDY: It's the detail I most admire. The plaster moulding! The carved balustrade! And the Edwardian bathroom!

KEITH: You didn't use the downstairs lavatory?

RODDY: I fancied a bit of a wander. I found this antique treasure. Bath with claw feet. Chipped enamel and yellow round the plughole.

KEITH: (*Deeply suspicious.*) Where was this bathroom?

RODDY: Top of the stairs. First right. You must know it. Oh, and best of all a genuine mahogany loo seat. They're very collectable.

KEITH: (*Appalled.*) You didn't collect it!

RODDY: Of course not. I sat on it.

KEITH: You sat on it!

RODDY: That's what it's for, isn't it? So much warmer and more comforting than plastic. I could've gone to sleep. I mean, I could've stayed there all night.
(*He sits, with his drink and cigar.*)

KEITH: No, you couldn't!

RODDY: I never thought we'd meet again. After Saint Tom's.
(*Pause.*)

KEITH: No.

RODDY: I never thought our paths would cross again.

KEITH: It seemed extremely unlikely.

RODDY: An outside chance! But it came up. A bit of luck.

KEITH: Was it?

RODDY: For me. I hope so... Dear old Saint Tom's College. Do you ever go back there?

KEITH: Never.

RODDY: No. Neither do I. Of course, we've come a long way since then.

KEITH: Yes. (*Moves towards the door.*) It's been nice chatting to you.

RODDY: (*Laughing.*) Liar!

KEITH: Excuse me?

RODDY: It hasn't been nice for you. Not chatting to me. I bet you hoped you'd never have to chat to me again.

KEITH: (*Moving towards the door.*) I'm sorry, I've got work to do...

RODDY: And I have someone who's trying to murder my reputation. A solicitor called Hanshaw. Of Hanshaw, Hawkish and Reeks.

KEITH: I can't possibly discuss anyone's case.

RODDY: You'll recognise him quite easily. Booming voice, red face, overblown carnation in the button-hole. Goes to the races in a tweed suit and a squashed hat. He's a fellow who raised money on empty houses with vanished owners. A President of the Rotary Club who mortgaged property he didn't happen to own.

KEITH: I knew we shouldn't have invited guests. You know perfectly well. I can't talk about forthcoming trials. It would be highly improper.

RODDY: (*He looks hard at KEITH.*) You know. Now I come to look at you, I can't think how I ever came to fancy you!

(*Long pause. KEITH moves tot he drinks table, pours himself a whisky, drinks.*)

You remember our times together at old Saint T's, don't you? You *do* remember?

KEITH: I recall you as a bit of a show off. Wore purple corduroy trousers, if I remember rightly.

RODDY: And swung both ways.

(*KEITH turns to look at him.*)

KEITH: I think the others will be wondering what's happened to us.

RODDY: No, they won't. Anyway, I'll look after Mizz Elspeth later. I can swing her way quite easily. And old Uncle's probably tucked up in bed, coping with his back. (*Stands.*) When we first met, you didn't swing any way at all. Just a pale, young schoolboy trying not to admit he was fascinated with purple corduroy trousers.

(*Pause.*)

KEITH: What do you want?

RODDY: I'm not asking much, Keith, darling. I'm just asking you to remember. You can do that, can't you? An act of imagination. Throw yourself back into the past. Meet young Keith, a boy with an interesting profile and no enemies. No friends either, come to that. A damp-handed stripling who would develop a nervous twitch when spoken to by a girl, and run for cover.

KEITH: That's a ridiculous exaggeration!

RODDY: Probably. But the truth's even funnier. Friday night. Do you remember? In the JCR. The rugger buggers screaming after some long-forgotten victory and a couple of third-year students vomiting on the floor. And then Keith, involved in his first genuine, no holds barred, old English piss-up, soliciting my favours! 'I've wanted to say this all year. I do love you, Roddy!' (*Pause.*)

KEITH: Why are you telling me all this?

RODDY: Unnecessary, do you think? I'm sure you haven't forgotten. The night you got extraordinarily lucky.

KEITH: Was I lucky?

RODDY: I'll say you were. Do yourself justice. It wasn't just the Snowballs and the Newcastle Brown. It was that clear little profile. Those eyes full of terror and desire. Of course, I didn't know how you'd end up. I was just engaged on an act of absurd generosity. But it's paid off.

KEITH: How?

RODDY: You're going to help me.

KEITH: Am I?

RODDY: Oh, yes. You know what that four-letter fellow, that pompous prick, that bucket shop lawyer, that button-holed, squash-hatted, purple-nosed, snake in the grass Hanshaw is planning to do at the trial...?

KEITH: I can't discuss...

RODDY: Only wants to put it all down to his accountant. Only says that I supplied him with all the info about the houses. Only tell the world that Roddy was the brains behind the whole fraudulent cock-up. It won't help him, of course. He's off to a long holiday in an open prison. But he wants me dragged along behind the black van. In irons! That's what he wants, Keith. So, in return for past favours, would you mind...?

KEITH: Doing what?

RODDY: Do I have to spell it out? You're the Judge, aren't you? All I'm asking you to do is keep me out of it. (*KEITH stands.*)

KEITH: I can't.

RODDY: Can't you?

KEITH: I can't keep out evidence if it's relevant. I don't know what the prosecution's going to say. Or the defence. Even if... Even if I wanted to help you. It's impossible!

RODDY: Sorry, darling. I don't believe it. You'll just have to get that ingenious brain of yours working. You were quite an ingenious little thing if I remember. And so enthusiastic you didn't even notice the smell of the girl I'd had in the afternoon. You can do anything you want, Keith. Otherwise...

KEITH: Otherwise what?

RODDY: I might start talking about the old days. Give that old Uncle Fred Dotteridge another dinner time story. So you'll do it for me, won't you, darling?

(*RODDY moves towards KEITH and kisses him. Then he moves away and out of one of the doors. KEITH stands, looking after him, then he gathers up his papers and goes quickly, leaving the lamp on the table lit. FRED's head appears over the back of the sofa. He gets up slowly and goes to the drinks table. Pours himself a drink. Turns to the audience.*)

FRED: Blimey!

End of Act One.

ACT TWO

Light downstage. We hear the March from 'Aida' as KEITH, FRED and ELSPETH enter in procession, impressively robed as Judges, KEITH in scarlet, FRED and ELSPETH in black Judges' robes. As they get centre stage they bow to the audience. Then KEITH moves away into upstage shadows. FRED watches him go for a beat then, in a downstage pool of light, speaks.

FRED: There he goes. Keith's trying crime. He's got the best job, of course. Crime deals with the weakness of mankind, the reality of life on earth, the curse of misfortune and the struggle for happiness. Cases about the human condition. Not some rigmarole about penalty clauses and certificates of completion, draught exclusion and sanitary conditions. When I asked the great monument of pomposity, the QC, or queer customer, appearing for the Borough Council exactly what provisions of the Public Health Act he was talking about it took him an entire afternoon to tell me. I wrote him a little note. 'Dear Pomposity QC,' I wrote to him. 'Do you think I *really* want to know about the Public Health Acts? You know what I wish – I wish to God I'd never asked you the bloody question.' I tore the note up, of course. Sitting on the bench you have to preserve a certain aloofness. When it's a fight between the Builders and the Borough Council it's easy to be impartial. It takes, in fact, very little effort not to give a tuppenny toss who wins or loses.
(FRED sighs with resignation and goes. ELSPETH, wearing her judge's wig and gown, stays in the downstage pool of light.)
ELSPETH: Family life! Family life is an enigma to those of us who deal with matrimonial cases. It's an enigma wrapped in a mystery. This husband who enjoyed sitting in cake for instance. A middle-of-the-road middle manager of a company selling world religions on the

Internet. Godseekers Dot Com. Attractive wife, two intelligent children at church schools loaded with GCSEs. Mortgage almost paid off. Well, when his wife asked him how he got on with his psychiatrist he said, 'Wonderful. She sits on cake far more prettily than you do.' All the same, they seem to be still determined to save the marriage. His wife's prepared to sit on cake for the sake of the children. Well. That's family life at its most horrific. Can you wonder that, as far as I'm concerned, I want nothing to do with it!

(*ELSPETH goes.*)

(*Light upstage, where the furniture now acts as a courtroom where KEITH is sitting as the Judge. CASSANDRA and DAWLISH, both in wigs and gowns, are on opposite sides. SWIVER is with CASSANDRA. BYRON is downstage, sitting with his back to the audience in what represents a dock. INSPECTOR DACRE is standing, being examined by DAWLISH. The jury is the audience.*)

DAWLISH: Detective Inspector Dacre. You and Detective Sergeant Brian arrested young Byron Johnson. Did you travel with him in the car to the station…?

DACRE: I did, my Lord.

DAWLISH: How long did the journey take?

DACRE: About fifteen minutes, my Lord. There were road works.

DAWLISH: Did he start talking…?

CASSANDRA: (*Sitting.*) Before he was cautioned…

KEITH: Miss Cresswell.

CASSANDRA: (*Rising.*) Yes, my Lord.

(*DAWLISH sits.*)

KEITH: If you wish to make an objection, it's customary to do it standing, and in a clear voice.

CASSANDRA: I understand that, my Lord.

KEITH: Good! I'm glad you do. Now. What was it you wished to say?

CASSANDRA: I wish to say… I object to evidence of what my client said before a caution.

KEITH: I'm sure Mr Marston Dawlish, with his considerable experience of these matters, has that well in mind. Yes, Mr Marston Dawlish…

DAWLISH: (*Rising.*) Thank you, my Lord. Detective Inspector, when, if ever, did you caution the defendant?

DACRE: On his arrest, my Lord.

KEITH: On his arrest. Yes. That is exactly what I would have expected.

(*CASSANDRA sits, says in an audible whisper to SWIVER.*)

CASSANDRA: Bastard!

DAWLISH: And in the car...

DACRE: He told us that he'd gone to Jubilee Road to see the dead man, Winston Jardine. He said they quarrelled.

DAWLISH: Did he say what they quarrelled about?

DACRE: I understood that the defendant resented Jardine's staying at the restaurant with his mother.

DAWLISH: Did he tell you how the quarrel ended?

DACRE: He said he lost his temper and stabbed Winston Jardine with a knife, my Lord.

KEITH: A knife he had brought with him?

DACRE: Yes, my Lord.

DAWLISH: Inspector. When you reached the station, did you and DS Brian make a note of that conversation?

DACRE: We did, my Lord.

DAWLISH: And in the presence of the station officer, was that note read over to Byron Johnson?

DACRE: We gave it to him and he read it himself.

DAWLISH: And did he sign it?

DACRE: He did, my Lord.

DAWLISH: And is that the statement?

DACRE: It is, my Lord.

DAWLISH: My Lord. I have no further questions. (*He sits.*)

KEITH: Miss Cresswell. Have you any questions for this officer?

CASSANDRA: (*Rising.*) I certainly have, my Lord. (*To DACRE.*) Are you honestly telling us that Byron Johnson, as soon as he got into the car, poured out his heart to you two police officers?

KEITH: By 'pouring out his heart', I take it you mean confessing his guilt, Miss Cresswell?

CASSANDRA: Whatever you call it. Are you telling this jury that a young black boy would have such a touching trust in this town's police force as to start talking immediately...?

DACRE: He had no reason not to trust us.

CASSANDRA: Inspector Dacre. Do you honestly mean that...?

KEITH: Presumably he does, Miss Cresswell. Or he wouldn't have said it.

CASSANDRA: Inspector Dacre. Will you tell the jury how many complaints have been made, during the last year, of racist behaviour by the local police?

DACRE: There are always a large number of complaints against the police, my Lord.

KEITH: (*A wintry smile at the jury.*) There are always a large number of complaints against judges, too.

(*DAWLISH laughs heartily. Sound of laughter offstage.*)

Have you any *relevant* questions, Miss Cresswell?

CASSANDRA: Certainly, my Lord. Detective Inspector, were you in charge of the case which led to the arrest of Joseph Perkin?

KEITH: Did you say Parkin?

CASSANDRA: Perkin, my Lord.

DACRE: I was in overall charge, yes.

CASSANDRA: Was he assaulted by the officers who arrested him?

DACRE: That was his complaint.

CASSANDRA: Quite a successful complaint, wasn't it? Did he bring an action and receive twenty thousand pounds' damages for false imprisonment against the police?

DACRE: I believe the case was settled, my Lord.

CASSANDRA: You mean, the police gave in and agreed to pay twenty thousand...?

DAWLISH: (*Rising wearily.*) My Lord. You asked if my learned friend had any *relevant* questions...

KEITH: Yes. Miss Cresswell. I take it you are about to suggest that your client was in some way assaulted by these two police officers?

CASSANDRA: No, my Lord.

KEITH: (*Raises his eyebrows.*) You are not...? Then what on earth's the relevance of this Perkins...?

CASSANDRA: Perkin, my Lord. The relevance of it is that, knowing the reputation of the police among the Black Community, Byron would have been highly unlikely to confide in them as soon as he got into the car.

KEITH: (*Weary again.*) Is that your *best* point, Miss Cresswell?

CASSANDRA: Not quite, my Lord...

KEITH: Then perhaps... (*He looks towards a clock.*) Ten-thirty tomorrow morning, members of the jury.

(*Light change. The courtroom characters go in darkness as muzak plays.*)

(*Light downstage. ELSPETH and RODDY are drinking together in the hotel bar.*)

RODDY: You didn't mind. Meeting here, I mean?

ELSPETH: Not really. We're not supposed to haunt bars, or mix with the public. Keith wouldn't approve...

RODDY: Keith! (*Small laugh.*) I don't think we have to worry about Keith any more. (*Pause.*) I want to give you a bit of good news. You know I've been going through a bit of a bad patch lately. Not from any fault of my own...

ELSPETH: (*Smiles.*) When haven't you been going through a bad patch...? It's something I've grown to love about you.

RODDY: (*Serious and rather pompous for a change.*) I have asked you here, Elspeth. To offer you security.

(*Pause. She looks at him with growing dread.*)

ELSPETH: Offer me *what?*

RODDY: Marriage.

ELSPETH: I spend my days disentangling marriages. Sorting out the consequences of furtive infidelities. Doing my best for the kids. Deciding who gets the custody of the digital television. You think I want to go home to that? I want to go home to a quiet evening of irresponsible and, if possible, spectacular sex.

RODDY: (*Ignoring this.*) Someone's put me onto a cottage. You'd really love it. I'd be at the office in the daytime, of

course. And a few boring dinners with the local big-wigs.
Lions, Freemasons, Elks. All those sort of King of the
Jungle rituals. But you could get the garden going. And
you'd have the dogs. They'll keep your hands full...

ELSPETH: (*Appalled.*) I'd have the dogs...!

RODDY: Jack Russell, a Labrador and a cocker spaniel.
Remember...

ELSPETH: I remember. Muddy paws on my white trousers.
Muzzles pressed into my crotch. You mean, I'd have the
dogs all day?

RODDY: Well, you wouldn't want to keep your job, would
you?

ELSPETH: Wouldn't I?

RODDY: I mean, I'd feel a bit ridiculous married to a judge.

ELSPETH: How ridiculous would I feel... As a sort of
perpetual kennel maid?

RODDY: But you're always complaining. About your job.

ELSPETH: At least it keeps me in touch with people going
through bad patches... How did you emerge from yours,
now we're on the subject?

RODDY: I just thought of a scheme for solving my particular
troubles.

ELSPETH: *You* thought of it?

RODDY: As a matter of fact, it was one of your Judge chaps
gave me the idea.

ELSPETH: Not Uncle Fred?

RODDY: No. The other one.

ELSPETH: (*Astonished.*) Keith! At dinner, as far as I can
remember, Keith was toying with the idea of cracking
down on careless driving by means of mandatory life
sentences or some such nonsense and Fred was recycling
his old jokes. What did Keith tell you...?

RODDY: Something he said helped me solve a certain legal
problem. I don't think I should say any more at the
moment, except... (*A charming smile.*) What about it, old
girl? Why don't you relax a bit and marry me!

ELSPETH: (*Looks at her watch.*) I'd better get back to dinner
in the lodgings. Your friend Keith doesn't like us being

late. (*She gets up, starts to go.*) Life in the Family Court may be pretty good hell at times. But, in my view, Roddy, it beats looking after dogs.

(*She goes. Lights fade.*)

(*CASSANDRA and SWIVER enter downstage. She's robed, carrying her wig. They are on their way to court.*)

CASSANDRA: That bloody man!

SWIVER: We know him well down here, Miss Cresswell. Quite frankly, we dread him coming.

CASSANDRA: I just hope I got the point over to the jury.

SWIVER: You did manfully, Miss Cresswell. I have to say that for you.

CASSANDRA: How about...I did womanfully?

SWIVER: Sorry. It's the correctness, I know. I can't seem to keep up with it.

CASSANDRA: I thought not.

SWIVER: And that Marston Dawlish. I'd call him cheap! Flirting with the judge. Smooching up to him, if you want my honest opinion.

CASSANDRA: (*Looks disapproving.*) Womanful behaviour? (*Pause.*) I'm going to ditch this judge.

SWIVER: (*Doubtful.*) You're sure...?

CASSANDRA: I've made up my mind. We'll get the jury to loathe him as much as we do.

SWIVER: And how do we manage that?

CASSANDRA: Egg him on. Lead him on to behave even more like a cold-blooded, hard-hearted, merciless bully.

SWIVER: You mean, manfully?

CASSANDRA: You've got it, Mr Swiver.

(*During the above scene, the upstage area has been entered by the courtroom characters, including DACRE. He is standing in the witness position. CASSANDRA moves upstage, putting on her wig, takes her place in court, standing, but instead of addressing the witness, she's having a quick consultation with SWIVER, who has taken his place behind her. KEITH is restless and irritable.*)

KEITH: Miss Cresswell. We can't all wait on your convenience.

(*CASSANDRA takes no notice.*)

Miss Cresswell!

(*CASSANDRA finishes talking to SWIVER. Then she turns and smiles at KEITH.*)

You are keeping the court waiting!

CASSANDRA: Oh, I'm sure the jury won't mind that, my Lord. (*She looks at the audience.*) A few more minutes for us may mean the whole of young Byron Johnson's life…

KEITH: (*Furious.*) Miss Cresswell…!

(*CASSANDRA ignores him and turns quickly to the witness.*)

CASSANDRA: Inspector. I want to get this perfectly clear. You say that this so-called confession was first made to you two officers in the car when you arrested Byron…

DACRE: He said it in the car. Yes.

CASSANDRA: In the back seat?

DACRE: Yes.

CASSANDRA: Sitting between you…?

DACRE: Yes.

CASSANDRA: This touching scene wasn't immortalised on video?

DACRE: There was no video, no.

CASSANDRA: It wasn't recorded on tape…?

DACRE: No.

CASSANDRA: Did you choose to have this conversation in the car so that there should be no record of it?

KEITH: There was a record of it later, Miss Cresswell. Don't you remember?

CASSANDRA: I'm coming to that, if your Lordship will allow me. (*To DACRE.*) So! This boy is admitting to murder… And there's no solicitor, no recording machine… Nothing!

DACRE: That is right… But…

CASSANDRA: But you wrote out a record of what you *say* you remembered… With your Sergeant?

DACRE: (*To KEITH.*) Immediately on arrival at the station… My Lord.

CASSANDRA: And was Byron present when you made up that document?

DACRE: He wasn't present. No.

KEITH: Miss Cresswell. You used the expression 'made up'. Can we be clear about this. Are you saying that these officers invented the conversation in the car?

CASSANDRA: I thank your Lordship. Your Lordship puts it far more clearly than I did.

KEITH: I am merely trying to discover what your case is. Of course, you'll deal with the fact that your client read over and signed the record...

CASSANDRA: My Lord. The prosecution in this case is ably represented by my learned friend, Mr Dawlish. I'm sure he can manage without your Lordship's assistance.

KEITH: (*Furious.*) Miss Cresswell! That was an outrageous remark!

CASSANDRA: Then, of course, the jury will disregard it. (*To the witness.*) So, the first Byron knew of any sort of record of the conversation in the car was this document? (*She holds up her copy.*)

DACRE: Which he signed.

CASSANDRA: If you could call that a signature...

DACRE: It's a bit of a scrawl...

CASSANDRA: A complete scrawl, isn't it?

DACRE: If you say so...

CASSANDRA: Quite illegible...?

DACRE: It's difficult to make out what it says. Yes.

KEITH: Perhaps like the signatures of a good many doctors, and businessmen...?

CASSANDRA: Inspector. We're not talking about doctors and business tycoons. We're talking about a seventeen-year-old boy. Did you read it aloud to him before he signed it?

DACRE: No.

CASSANDRA: Why not?

DACRE: Because we gave him ample time to read it to himself.

CASSANDRA: Inspector Dacre. Are you sure Byron read this statement?

DACRE: Quite sure.

CASSANDRA: Do you swear that on your oath...?

KEITH: He's already on his oath, Miss Cresswell.

CASSANDRA: Do you swear it?

DACRE: I have done so. Yes.

CASSANDRA: And do you swear these notes were read over by Byron?

DACRE: I saw him read them through. Yes.

CASSANDRA: In your presence?

DACRE: And Sergeant Brian. And the station officer.

CASSANDRA: That's completely untrue, isn't it?

(*Pause. KEITH seems about to say something, but thinks better of it.*)

Didn't you realise, Inspector? Byron Johnson can't read.

(*Light change. The light fades as the court empties and comes up as the furniture is moved into the lodgings. HUBERT is standing as FRED comes into the room.*)

HUBERT: Feeling a bit better now, are we?

FRED: I have to say, Hubert. Your cure was quite miraculous.

HUBERT: I told you, didn't I? It's the toes. They're the nerve centre of all our ills.

FRED: I wouldn't say it was the toes exactly.

Pause.

HUBERT: Interesting case today, was it?

FRED: I don't do interesting cases any more. (*Depressed.*) Building contracts.

HUBERT: That's all they'll give you. After you had that trouble...

FRED: Not my trouble. Theirs. The star-crossed lovers.

HUBERT: They shouldn't've done it.

FRED: Probably not. (*Pause.*) Verona was the Cowslip Meadow Estate, a race track for stolen cars and a local drug market. The balcony was cracked concrete fifteen floors up and they had sex on it. Juliet was fourteen, like in the play. He was seventeen and happened to be her brother. When the social worker found out and called it incest, Juliet panicked and said Romeo forced her. There was no Friar Lawrence to administer death-like drugs, so

he turned up before me at the Old Bailey. The jury
consisted of right wing hangers and floggers and the left
wing politically correct.
A deadly combination! I had to sentence a boy I knew
hadn't committed rape. His eyes were full of terror. What
did I give him? Probation? Community Service?
A suspended sentence.

HUBERT: Keith wouldn't have done that.

FRED: I don't think so! The tabloids were down on me like
a ton of bricks. 'Dotty Dotteridge.' 'His Raving Loony
Lordship.' 'Pat On The Head For A Young Rapist.' That's
when I was taken off crime.

HUBERT: I heard your clerks talking. Keith's dead set on
convicting that black boy.

FRED: I expect he is.

HUBERT: And as for that lady brief... He'd like to give
her a life sentence.

FRED: I can think of very few people Keith wouldn't like to
give life sentences to.
(*Pause.*)

HUBERT: I'll go and give Mother a hand. Tonight it's
moussaka à la grècque. Baked jam roll to follow...she's
done it for you special.
(*HUBERT goes. FRED gets up, mixes himself a strong
whisky. He sings to himself, in a faint American accent, 'They
Can't That Away From Me.' KEITH enters, in a bad mood.
FRED stops singing. He mixes a drink for KEITH.*)

FRED: Had a good day?

KEITH: (*Sits.*) An infuriating day!

FRED: I'll give you a drink...

KEITH: Thank you.

FRED: So what was wrong? People protesting their
innocence? It's so irritating – when people don't want to
go to prison.
(*FRED hands KEITH his drink.*)

KEITH: (*He drinks.*) There's a certain Mizz Cassandra
Cresswell...

FRED: Let me guess... Count One against her. She's a
woman.

KEITH: Your powers of deduction are extraordinary.

FRED: Count Two. She's appearing for the defence.

KEITH: I know exactly what she's doing.

FRED: Trying to get her client off? They will, you know. Given the slightest encouragement.

KEITH: She was trying to make the jury dislike me.

FRED: Did she have to try terribly hard?

KEITH: It was a cheap advocate's trick.

FRED: Because you're naturally so lovable?

KEITH: Because her man's clearly guilty.

FRED: A man? He's a youth, a teenager. Perhaps…a child.

KEITH: A friend of yours?

FRED: (*Gets up and pours himself another whisky.*) Unfortunately not. I saw him as they led me down a passage. Towards the building contracts. The door of your court had been left open. You were graciously acknowledging the servile bows of the legal profession. I caught a glimpse of a boy in the dock. He looked…amazed. As though he were an explorer who had come upon a strange tribe performing some obscure ritual…

KEITH: A boy? A killer!

FRED: He's innocent. Until the jury come back and find him guilty.

KEITH: That's a legal fiction!

FRED: Call it an act of faith.

KEITH: That's all it is.

FRED: What sort of faith would you prefer? Original sin? Damnation at birth? The presumption of guilt?

KEITH: They say he can't read. (*Pause.*) I suspect he's a liar.

FRED: Even liars tell the truth occasionally. It's for the prosecution to prove he's lying.

KEITH: (*Sarcastic.*) Uncle Fred. I'm enormously grateful to you for teaching me the basic principles of English law.

FRED: That's a lie.

KEITH: What?

FRED: You're not grateful to me at all!

KEITH: You can be extremely irritating!

FRED: Now you're telling me the truth.

KEITH: Anyway. Mizz Cresswell…

FRED: Who decided to ditch you?

KEITH: She'll live to regret it. (*He stands.*) I'm going to get that jury on my side.

FRED: And I know how you'll do it.

KEITH: How?

FRED: Obvious, old sport. You're going to start buttering them up.

(*KEITH stands still for a moment. Looks at FRED.*)

KEITH: You know. I think you're right…

(*Suddenly, unexpectedly, he smiles. He goes, passing ELSPETH on her way in.*)

ELSPETH: He looks happy.

FRED: Very happy…suddenly.

(*She goes to pour herself a drink.*)

ELSPETH: Back in sole possession of his loo seat.

FRED: Oh, better than that.

ELSPETH: It can't be the thought of dinner…?

FRED: Wendy's moussaka? I don't think so. In fact that's quite likely to wipe the smile off his face. No. He's looking forward to tomorrow morning.

ELSPETH: His murder?

FRED: That's right. Keith's murder. He's remembered how to kill the defence.

ELSPETH: (*She turns to look at him.*) How's that?

FRED: He's going to charm the jury. Have you ever seen Keith being charming?

ELSPETH: Has anyone?

FRED: Oh, I have. Absolutely terrifying. It's likely to strike terror into the heart of the bravest defender.

(*Light change. As FRED and ELSPETH go, light comes up on BYRON's trial, with KEITH presiding. CASSANDRA and DAWLISH take their places. KEITH is leaning forward, doing his best to be charming and flattering to the jury/audience.*)

KEITH: Members of the jury. I do hope you're comfortable. This courtroom's not too stuffy for you? It's acceptable, is it? Otherwise I can ask the usher to adjust the thermostat. And I hope your sandwiches were fresh and…appetising.

If you have any problem at all with your sandwiches, I do
hope you'll let the jury bailiff know. Then I shall attend to
the matter personally. (*Pause.*) As we go through this trial
together, you may have heard me interrupt Counsel
from time to time, and you might have thought...
(*Smiles.*) 'Why does his Lordship keep on interrupting?'
Well. Just let me say this. I have only been anxious to
make sure that the vital points are clear to you. We have
two barristers here. Mr Marston Dawlish and Miss...
er...Cresswell. But they don't have to decide this case.
Nor do I. It's your case, members of the jury. Please
remember that. *You* are by far the most important people
in this room!

SWIVER: (*To CASSANDRA.*) What's he up to?

CASSANDRA: Buttering up the jury. The creep!

KEITH: (*To the jury/audience.*) So, members of the jury.
Let us, you and I together, sit quietly and listen to the
evidence. After that, I'll have the great pleasure of
speaking to you again. Oh, and please do remember. Send
me a message if you have the slightest trouble on the
question of sandwiches. Yes, Mr Marston Dawlish.

DAWLISH: (*Rises.*) I'm grateful to your Lordship.
(*He turns to the witness box, where MR BREADWELL is
now standing. He is a fortyish, stressed teacher at a
comprehensive school.*)
George Henry Breadwell. Did you teach the defendant in
his last year at his secondary school, the Harold Wilson
Comprehensive?

BREADWELL: I did, my Lord... Until he left us.

DAWLISH: And when he left you, could he read?

BREADWELL: We certainly aim to equip our pupils with
the basic skills of literacy and numeracy...

DAWLISH: In the case of Byron Johnson, did you succeed?

BREADWELL: My Lord. We live in difficult times. So
many inspections. So many changes. We have tests to
see how we've done in tests and targets to discover how
we're meeting targets. It's very hard to concentrate on an
individual pupil and...

KEITH: (*Impatient.*) Never mind about all that. You were asked a simple question. Could the young man in the dock read when he left school?

BREADWELL: I believe so… Yes.

KEITH: (*Making a note.*) Yes. I believe so…

DAWLISH: It's fair to say the records show that he had some difficulty at primary school?

KEITH: That question shows the fairness one would expect of you, Mr Marston Dawlish.

BREADWELL: Reports were made on him and he was sent to an educational psychiatrist. When he left primary school, his reading was entered at Level Two.

KEITH: How many levels are there?

BREADWELL: Four. Level Four is the top, my Lord.

DAWLISH: And he was Two?

BREADWELL: Yes.

KEITH: So he wasn't bottom of the class. As we said in our day, didn't we, members of the jury? (*Smiles at the jury.*) I'm sure none of *you* ever deserved that title!
(*Faint laugh from the jury.*)

DAWLISH: After that he had another five years of schooling. Are you satisfied that he was basically literate when he left school?

BREADWELL: I think he was. Yes…
(*DAWLISH sits.*)

KEITH: (*Making another note.*) 'I think he was. Yes.' Have you any questions, Miss Cresswell?

CASSANDRA: (*Rising.*) A few, my Lord. Mr Breadwell. The Harold Wilson is not one of the most successful schools, is it?

BREADWELL: It's in…a difficult area. And as I was trying to explain, there've been so many changes and inspections…

CASSANDRA: And your school has had a bad inspectors' report?

BREADWELL: We've tried to put a few things right since then, but…

CASSANDRA: Did it become known as a 'sink school'?

BREADWELL: I've heard that said about us, yes.

CASSANDRA: So, are you reluctant to admit that you might have failed to teach one of your pupils to read? They might shut you down...

KEITH: Miss Cresswell. Are you suggesting this witness is committing perjury?

CASSANDRA: (*Airily.*) No, my Lord. Only that he's making the best of a bad job. (*To BREADWELL.*) Isn't it a fact that a significant number of pupils leave school unable to read? Are you sure that Byron Johnson wasn't one of those?

BREADWELL: I don't think he was.

KEITH: (*Heavy sigh.*) He's told us that, Miss Cresswell.

CASSANDRA: But he hasn't told us this. Isn't Level Two where all children who can't read without assistance are put automatically?

BREADWELL: (*Reluctantly.*) That's so. Yes...

CASSANDRA: So when he left primary school, he couldn't read without help?

KEITH: Miss Cresswell! He had another five years' schooling!

CASSANDRA: Oh. I'm so glad your Lordship reminded the jury of that. I'm extremely grateful to your Lordship.

KEITH: (*Angry.*) Miss Cresswell!

CASSANDRA: Five years later, how did Byron do in his GCSEs?

BREADWELL: He didn't.

CASSANDRA: Didn't?

BREADWELL: He didn't do them.

CASSANDRA: How did that come about?

BREADWELL: (*Sighs.*) He wasn't about at the time.

CASSANDRA: Was he frequently absent?

BREADWELL: Yes. Apparently. There were a good many calls to the mother. There's a note that he sometimes stayed away to help in the restaurant... At others...

CASSANDRA: He just stayed away! And when he did turn up...what do your records show?

BREADWELL: He was noisy in class. Inattentive. A short concentration span. But likeable when he was there.
(*CASSANDRA picks up a piece of paper, reads from it.*)

CASSANDRA: 'I understand that I do not have to say anything, but that it may harm my defence if I don't mention, when questioned, something which I later rely on in court...'

KEITH: The start of your client's confession statement! The jury will remember that extremely well, Miss Cresswell. (*He looks meaningfully at the jury.*)

CASSANDRA: Could Byron have read it, Mr Breadwell?

BREADWELL: (*Hesitant.*) That's a difficult one...

CASSANDRA: You mean, a difficult one for him to read...?

BREADWELL: I think... He might have needed some help.

CASSANDRA: And we know from the Police Inspector's evidence, that he got no help at all. Yes. Thank you, Mr Breadwell.

(*She sits. DAWLISH rises, a paper in his hand.*)

DAWLISH: Mr Breadwell. Miss Cresswell has read out a rather complicated part of Byron's confession statement. May I read out a simpler sentence... 'I stabbed Winston three times. I think I got him in the chest and twice in the stomach. I threw away the knife.' Now then, Mr Breadwell. Could Byron have read that?

(*Pause.*)

BREADWELL: I believe he could.

DAWLISH: Could he... Yes or no?

BREADWELL: Well. I would say... Yes.

KEITH: (*Making a note.*) 'I would say...yes.' (*He smiles at the witness for the first time.*) Thank you, Mr Breadwell. (*He smiles at the jury.*) Members of the jury. It's a little early, but perhaps you'd like to take your coffee break now?

(*Lights fade on the court.*)

(*Lights come up on the lodgings. FRED is asleep. We hear voices at the door. FRED wakes. HUBERT ushers RODDY in.*)

RODDY: I called in to see Elspeth.

FRED: She's having a bath. A ceremony of cleansing. She feels the need of it constantly. (*Pause.*) You and Keith, you must have enjoyed talking about old times...

RODDY: We were at Saint Tom's together...

FRED: Yes, of course! Just reminiscing?

RODDY: That sort of thing.

FRED: Happy days, were they?

RODDY: I enjoyed them.

FRED: And so did Keith, apparently. He must have found you totally fascinating...

RODDY: Perhaps. (*Modestly.*) I suppose I had a certain boyish charm.

FRED: I suppose you did. You're still boyish, of course. Perhaps less charming. (*Pause.*) What did you want Keith to do for you?

RODDY: What do you mean?

FRED: Nothing at all?

RODDY: (*Innocently.*) I honestly don't know what you're talking about.

FRED: 'Honestly.' The word that always precedes a thundering lie. Let me make a suggestion...

RODDY: If you like...

FRED: I don't like. I feel it's my duty to protect a defenceless judge.

RODDY: Keith? Defenceless?

FRED: Well. Perhaps not quite as defenceless as you hoped. Now, let me think. Ah, yes. There's a solicitor in this town. A pillar of society. Chairman of the Rotary. Steward at the races. In line for Mayor. And he's been raising loans on empty and abandoned houses.

RODDY: There's a lot about that in the local rag...

FRED: And suppose this ingenious lawyer, feeling a little lonely, wants a companion in the frame. Perhaps a crooked accountant?

RODDY: (*Looks at him, worried.*) *You're* trying the case?

FRED: Thank you, Roddy. But no. No, I'm not trying it. You were right. Keith was the judge for you to blackmail. He's doing the crime up here.

RODDY: (*Outraged.*) For me to *what?*

FRED: What would you rather call it? Perverting the course of justice? Demanding decisions with menaces? I could still draft an indictment.

RODDY: Keith's not going to complain!

FRED: But I might. And you can't put the screws on me, you know. I can't go to sleep now without counting my sexual experiences. Some regrettable, many foolish, some miraculous. So far as I remember, you never figure on the list. I never slept with you in a bed which smelt of another girl...

RODDY: Keith told you?

FRED: Not a word. He has a certain modesty.

RODDY: How do you know?

FRED: I have a good deal of trouble with my back...

RODDY: What's that got to do with it?

FRED: Don't worry your pretty head about that, Roddy. Take it from me. Your 'reminiscences' were heard by a most reliable witness. Another word from you on the subject to a living being and I'll be delighted to hand my evidence in at the local nick... I can't imagine any judge taking a favourable view.

(Pause. RODDY looks at him.)

RODDY: *(Shocked.)* That's blackmail!

FRED: Of course. Your special subject.

(ELSPETH enters.)

ELSPETH: *(To RODDY.)* Hubert told me you were here.

FRED: Goodbye, Roddy. I don't suppose you'll be staying for dinner.

(FRED goes.)

RODDY: Why did he say that?

ELSPETH: You never know. With Fred.

(Pause.)

RODDY: Do you think he fancies you?

ELSPETH: Would you mind?

RODDY: *(Avoiding the question.)* Quite honestly, Elspeth...

ELSPETH: What?

RODDY: Things haven't panned out quite as well as I expected.

ELSPETH: How surprising...

RODDY: I'm sorry to disappoint you... I mean, I came to talk to you about...what I suggested yesterday.

ELSPETH: *(Moves away from him.)* A cottage! Roses round the door! Dogs! I don't want to hear another word about your sexual fantasies.

RODDY: I'm glad you said that.

ELSPETH: Are you really?

RODDY: It makes it a bit easier.

ELSPETH: And you do like things to be made easy.

RODDY: I'm afraid all that I said. About the cottage and...

ELSPETH: The dogs!

RODDY: And, well, marriage... It's off the menu for the moment.

ELSPETH: Thank God for that!

RODDY: You mean...?

ELSPETH: I mean – at least things are back to normal.

RODDY: I'm afraid there's a bit of a bad patch ahead.

ELSPETH: That's exactly what I mean...

RODDY: So if... I don't know...if you still have any idea...

ELSPETH: Of course I have!

RODDY: Like...what, exactly?

ELSPETH: Like. I'll take you out to a Thai dinner. My clerk recommends the 'Midnight Garden'.

RODDY: I think that's an absolutely splendid scheme.

ELSPETH: Provided you promise me...

RODDY: Promise?

ELSPETH: Not to say anything serious. Just smile a lot. And tell small lies. You can manage that, can't you?

RODDY: No problem.

ELSPETH: See you then, in half an hour.

(*RODDY goes, passing FRED who is coming back into the room.*)

FRED: You're going out?

ELSPETH: For a Thai dinner.

FRED: With your friend?

ELSPETH: Who else?

FRED: The amusing accountant...

ELSPETH: Of course.

FRED: I'm afraid you might find he's...not quite so amusing.

ELSPETH: I know. He keeps prattling on about marriage and roses round the door and...

FRED: I don't mean that exactly.

ELSPETH: I'm glad. I thought I'd cured him of all that.

FRED: It's just that... I don't think he's an altogether reliable character.

ELSPETH: (*Delighted.*) That's better. That's what I want to hear.

FRED: Not just unreliable. Not simply charmingly irresponsible, but...

ELSPETH: Unscrupulous?

FRED: Yes.

ELSPETH: A really bad hat?

FRED: So my sources tell me.

ELSPETH: Who are your sources exactly?

FRED: I'm not at liberty to disclose...

ELSPETH: You meant that there's a skeleton in his cupboard?

FRED: And even emerging, from time to time, from the closet. With a considerable rattle.

ELSPETH: You make him sound rather interesting. I'll go and get changed for dinner. Thank you, Uncle Fred. Talking to you always does me a power of good.
(*She kisses him and goes, as she does so.*)

FRED: That's not exactly what I meant.
(*He pours himself a drink and then sits. Thoughtful. A little sad. KEITH enters, smiling and cheerful.*)

KEITH: Hallo, Uncle Fred. What're *you* up to?

FRED: I'm celebrating an anniversary.

KEITH: Your birthday?

FRED: (*Raising his glass.*) It's exactly two years since I last had sexual intercourse. You look unusually cheerful. Had a good day, Keith?

KEITH: Not bad. I think I've defused Mizz Cassandra Cresswell.

FRED: What did you do? Butter up the jury?

KEITH: Laid it on with a trowel!

FRED: Enquired tenderly about their sandwiches.

KEITH: How did you know?

FRED: I guessed.

KEITH: (*Going to the drinks table.*) I think they like me now.

FRED: There's no accounting for taste… (*Pause.*) Just saw your old friend Roddy Boyes.

KEITH: How was he…?

FRED: Going out with Elspeth. He'll be sorry to have missed you.

KEITH: Did you have much of a talk?

FRED: Not really.

(*KEITH looks relieved. Pause.*)

KEITH: You know we were at Saint Tom's together?

FRED: I know.

KEITH: Did he tell you?

FRED: You're not to worry your pretty little head about who told me.

KEITH: (*Looks at him, indignant.*) I beg your pardon?

FRED: It must've been pretty once. I suppose it must have been. What is it now? Hardly pretty. Prettiness has been carefully avoided. It's…what should we say? Distinguished. Judicial. Shall we say, daunting? (*Pause.*) So you reckon you've got the jury on your side?

KEITH: I think we can work together. Yes.

FRED: Work as a team. For the prosecution. And you're going to tell them to convict the boy?

KEITH: Not in so many words.

FRED: Oh. I know how you'll do it. 'It's a matter entirely for you, members of the jury. You're the sole judges of fact in this case. But can you really believe this man, who had the dead man's blood on his sleeve? Can you believe he's innocent? As I say, it's a matter for you. But quite honestly, "Pull the other one, it's got bells on it."' Repeat the defence and then yank an imaginary chain, hold your nose and flush it down the bog. (*He makes this gesture.*)

KEITH: I shan't do that.

FRED: But you'll say the rest.

KEITH: Words to that effect.

FRED: 'Lock this boy up for life, and here's your sandwiches.' Words to that effect.

KEITH: It's my duty to see that he doesn't get away with murder.

FRED: You'd be happy to see him convicted on a confession he couldn't read?

KEITH: The evidence that he couldn't read comes from his family.

FRED: So you'll tell the jury to ignore it.

KEITH: Not in so many words.

FRED: 'Evidence from his family and friends has to be treated with great caution, wouldn't you agree, members of the jury?' How many words is that?

KEITH: I shall make sure…that justice is done.

FRED: (*Suppressing anger, gets up.*) Justice! What's justice to you? Getting your way. Defusing an explosive girl in a wig. Making sure you get the verdict you've decided on…in your almighty prosecutor's mind!

KEITH: I shall conduct the case in my own way.

FRED: The delicate insertion of the boot. A quick jab and then, 'Guilty, my Lord.' That's music to your ears, isn't it, Keith?

KEITH: There is a certain satisfaction in defeating some spurious defence…

FRED: Which is what you intend to do… In the case of Byron Johnson?

KEITH: (*Looks at him in silence, then says.*) You love criminals, don't you?

FRED: No. I love people. It leads to endless difficulties.

KEITH: You love people who commit crimes.

FRED: Perhaps not hate them as much as you do, Keith.

KEITH: It's not a question of love or hate. It's a question of keeping the rules. What would happen if these people didn't fear the law?

FRED: You think we're here to scare them rigid?

KEITH: Fear's important. Fear makes them resist their natural instincts…

FRED: Which are?

KEITH: To cheat. To lie. To steal from each other. To give way to illegal lust…

FRED: Strangely enough I've found a lot of kindness…. People are naturally kind, helpful like…well, take Wendy, for instance.

KEITH: Wendy's a case in point! Wendy might have turned into a perfectly decent cook if only you'd put the fear of God into her.

FRED: And speaking personally... I haven't found it particularly difficult to go to more or less straight....

KEITH: Of course not! You're comfortable. Well fed. Nicely housed and in a warm judge's lodging. It's not hard to be honest on a full stomach.

FRED: Good, Keith. Very good. You're coming on! You recognise crime is the result of poverty.

KEITH: It's not our business to ask what it's the result of.... Insufficient weaning...unhappy childhood...quarrels with stepfather... Being dropped on the head when young. We've had it all, haven't we, in a long, whining, endless mitigation? We're here to make them all understand...as night follows day, crime leads to punishment. You broke the mould, Fred. When you let off your young rapist.

FRED: He wasn't a rapist. It wasn't even a crime.

KEITH: You mean incest isn't a crime? Sex with an underage girl isn't a crime? If you live in a world where nothing's a crime, what's the point of being a decent, honest, law abiding citizen?

FRED: (*Interrupting.*) I suppose what you did was a crime. Technically speaking. When were you at old Saint Tom's? Mid-sixties, was it?

KEITH: I have no idea what you mean...

FRED: In those days there was still some arcane and superstitious provision of our great criminal law. 'Gross indecency.' The one that potted Oscar Wilde. Wasn't it still lurking in the shadows somewhere, when you were at old Saint Tom's? I seem to remember defending two men who'd been found in an attitude of unusual friendliness under Waterloo Bridge. And the old Recorder of London, when he sent them away for two years, said, very seriously, 'You two men have been found guilty of a terrible crime. A ghastly crime! An act which has been cursed down the centuries. Which makes strong women vomit and men faint!' he said. 'And what

makes it so much *worse*, you chose to do it under one of
the most *beautiful* bridges in London!' Then he added,
'You two men should pull yourselves together!' Don't
you worry, Keith. The law's changed. They can't get you
now. That must be something of a relief. All the same,
it'll make a cracking good story.
(*Pause.*)

KEITH: What do you mean...exactly?

FRED: Not for general audiences, of course. To small
and select gatherings, of consenting QCs. A few judges
after dinner in the Benchers' smoking room. Over lunch
with dear old Tredgold from the Lord Chancellor's
office. Keith Craxton's great love affair with a dubious
accountant. I suppose it'll go down in the files, together
with my unfortunate dalliance with the quality of mercy.
'No longer top quality judge material.'
(*KEITH gets up, goes to the drinks table, pours himself another
whisky.*)

KEITH: I could say... I don't know what you're talking
about.

FRED: But you won't, will you, Keith? You won't try to get
away with any spurious defence...
(*Pause. KEITH goes back to his seat.*)

KEITH: He told you...?

FRED: Don't worry! I've shut him up, put the fear of the
law on him. The only chap who's likely to pass on the
glorious news is...

KEITH: You?

FRED: Exactly. (*Pause.*) It's funny when you think of it.

KEITH: Funny...?

FRED: We three, sitting down to Wendy's cassoulet, and
I was the only one who hadn't been rogered by Roddy
Boyes. Doesn't that strike you as comic?

KEITH: No.

FRED: It should be good for a laugh. In the Bar Mess...
(*Pause. KEITH looks at him and finally says.*)

KEITH: What do you want?

FRED: A fair trial, for that boy...

KEITH: What do you mean…a fair trial?

FRED: Oh, Keith. My dear old sport. Have you forgotten? Withdraw the boot. Don't drop heavy hints to the jury. Let them decide about the family's evidence for themselves. Put the defence as clearly as the prosecution. Don't cheat him on his life. That's all.

KEITH: This is an entirely criminal conversation.

FRED: There's a bit of a criminal in all of us.

KEITH: It's blackmail!

FRED: More or less.

KEITH: Perverting the course of justice!

FRED: Let's say…perverting the course of *in*justice.
(*Pause.*)

KEITH: It won't work, Fred.

FRED: I think it's working beautifully.

KEITH: It won't work because you haven't got the guts for it.

FRED: What do you mean?

KEITH: However I sum up in Johnson… You're never going to spread that story about me.

FRED: Why not?

KEITH: Because you couldn't bear to. Your bleeding heart would get in the way. The quality of your mercy would just about paralyse you. You haven't got the guts to punish. So… You couldn't bear to punish me.

FRED: Are you sure?

KEITH: Of course I'm sure. You couldn't even pot a boy for raping his sister.

FRED: It wasn't rape. Not even…a serious crime.

KEITH: Not a serious crime? Just a bit of a joke. Nothing's serious to you, is it? The world's not a serious place. The Law Courts are a delightful tea party, where you can make old jokes and be nice to people. So you'd find some excuse for me. A comfortable cushion of mitigating circumstances. 'Poor old Keith. He may go out of his way to pot the customers in the dock, but perhaps he can't help it. It's all down to his genes, or inadequate breast feeding. So I won't punish him after all. I'll let him off with a joke.'

FRED: Don't count on it. I warn you. Don't count on it for a moment. I can be a bit of a bitch at times.

(*HUBERT comes in.*)

HUBERT: Are you two Lordships coming in to dinner?

FRED: Of course. We've had a hard day judging people.

(*FRED takes KEITH's arm.*)

Come along, old sport. There are worse things in the world than Wendy's cooking.

(*They go. HUBERT is tidying up the glasses as ELSPETH enters, dressed to go out to dinner with RODDY.*)

ELSPETH: I meant to tell you, Hubert. I'll be out for dinner.

HUBERT: Can't say I blame you. Where're you going?

ELSPETH: Some Thai place. It's been recommended...

HUBERT: He seems nice enough. That young man of yours.

ELSPETH: (*Appalled.*) Nice? Did you say nice...? (*As she goes.*) I'll have to work on him...

(*Light change as HUBERT follows her out.*)

(*Light comes up on the court. KEITH is in the middle of his summing up.*)

KEITH: Members of the jury. You may think that in the particular area of this town where Winston kept on his flat, he may have had many enemies. Quarrels and vendettas may have broken out, about drug dealing or who knows what other doubtful transactions. Did someone, someone we know nothing about, come into the room, apparently unlocked, and stab him to death? Young Byron certainly called on him, and was stained with Winston's blood. You must seriously consider the possibility that that occurred when he knelt down to see what injuries Winston had received. You may not feel that it's a conclusive evidence of guilt. You may also feel some doubt about the interview with the police. Apparently it took place in the car, and Miss Cresswell has suggested that was because no recording could be made and there is, indeed, no corroboration of Byron's alleged confession. It was certainly not read out to him. You have heard a good deal of evidence from his family

and friends to the effect that Byron was, and is, to all intents and purposes, illiterate. The evidence of… (*Searches through his papers.*) Breadwell. You remember the schoolmaster? He told us he thought Byron Johnson couldn't have read part of the statement, at least. You may find his evidence hesitant and contradictory. To convict in this case, you must be sure of guilt. In all the circumstances, can you be certain, can you be sure, that this young boy murdered an older man, his mother's lover? It's a matter for you, of *course*, members of the jury. But I join with Miss Cresswell in asking you to remember this. If you have a doubt, young Byron Johnson is entitled to the benefit of the doubt. Please retire now. Take your time…and I will see that the jury bailiff provides you with suitable refreshment.
(*KEITH smiles. DAWLISH, who has been listening in amazement, now whispers audibly.*)

DAWLISH: Bloody hell!
(*Light fades upstage.*)
(*Downstage CASSANDRA appears with SWIVER. She is carrying her wig. They're on their way down to the cells.*)

CASSANDRA: This is always the worst part.

SWIVER: Waiting for the jury?

CASSANDRA: Visiting the client in the cells, while you're waiting for a verdict. I never quite know what to say.

SWIVER: 'See you again in about fourteen years,' I suppose you could say.

CASSANDRA: (*Smiling.*) 'Win a few, lose a few.'

SWIVER: Although… We're still in with a chance. Quite honestly.

CASSANDRA: (*Hardly daring to hope.*) Do you really think so?

SWIVER: I never expected to live so long as to hear Mr Justice Keith Craxton sum up for an acquittal!
(*They exit.*)
(*Light on the lodgings. FRED is sorting out papers and putting them into his briefcase. ELSPETH is mixing vodka, Galliano and orange juice in a cocktail shaker.*)

FRED: Cocktails?

ELSPETH: Something different. To cheer us up.

FRED: I was going to ask you. How was the Thai restaurant?

ELSPETH: Lonely.

FRED: What?

ELSPETH: Extremely lonely.

FRED: I'm sorry.

ELSPETH: I sat there in solitary splendour. Closely watched by a plastic elephant and the gilded model of a temple dancer. I breathed in the spicy and exotic smell of West Yorkshire. At any moment I expected him to come in breathless with apologies, run his finger through his hair in a boyish manner and order Moo Par, Prik Kapon – stir-fried pork with the royal orchid mixed starter.

FRED: And when he came?

ELSPETH: He didn't come. I rang him at home. I rang his office. Roddy Boyes has vanished. Into thin air.
(*Pause.*)

FRED: He would have gone... sooner or later.

ELSPETH: I know.

FRED: You shouldn't miss him.

ELSPETH: It's not just him. I sat there, in the Thai restaurant, and I saw it. The gulf between Judges and the judged. We took it on ourselves to judge other people and we became strangers to them. I tried to shout out to him – across the great divide. To tell him that I didn't want anyone respectable and boring. I wanted an impossible charmer... But he couldn't believe me and ran away. Leaving me... with nothing very much at all...

FRED: There's a lot left for you.

ELSPETH: How much exactly?

FRED: A lot. To be thankful for.

ELSPETH: What?

FRED: (*With great affection.*) You and I together. Drinking whisky, playing backgammon, trying not to be depressed by Keith. Doing our best to solve other people's problems. Not a bad way of life, Elspeth.

ELSPETH: A Judge's way.

FRED: Not too bad, under the circumstance.

(*She smiles at him.*)

ELSPETH: No. Not too bad. (*Pause. And then with regret.*) Perhaps it was seeing us all together that did it. I should never have asked him to dinner.

FRED: Oh, don't say that... I think that evening was a resounding success.

ELSPETH: (*Incredulous.*) You mean you enjoyed it?

FRED: Enormously! And Keith's never been quite the same since...

(*Pause.*)

ELSPETH: Do you think Keith's ill?

FRED: Keith's never ill. There's no known disease that dares attack him.

ELSPETH: While I waited I read the evening paper. It looked as though Keith's summing up in the murder was extremely favourable to the defence.

FRED: Odd, isn't it? I saw that too.

ELSPETH: Didn't it surprise you?

FRED: In a way. Although we had been having a little talk – about the presumption of innocence.

ELSPETH: That couldn't have had the slightest effect on him.

FRED: No, of course not. You're absolutely right.

(*Pause. ELSPETH looks at him, then takes his drink to him.*)

ELSPETH: Uncle Fred. Have you been up to something?

FRED: What a suspicious mind you have. I'm entirely innocent. Until proven guilty.

(*ELSPETH comes and sits beside him, smiles at him, puts a hand on his knee.*)

ELSPETH: Drink up. You need it. Otherwise a long journey with Keith would be like an operation without an anaesthetic.

(*They raise their glasses. They drink to each other, smiling together.*)

(*Downstage in a pool of light, BYRON enters, reading a newspaper. He shouts at someone offstage.*)

BYRON: I'm in it! I'm in the *Advertiser*...! 'Restaurant owner's son acquitted of murder. Byron Johnson (seventeen) of Bammy's Restaurant, Lansbury Road, was found not guilty by the unanimous verdict of the jury. Mr Justice Craxton discharged Byron when they returned after an hour's retirement. Last night, Byron was back serving the customers. At Bammy's... The Friday Night Special Black Crabs Baked!' It weren't'! (*Laughs.*) It was Squab Pie, wasn't it...? The old *Advertiser* got it wrong again!

(*Light fades quickly on BYRON and, at the same time, goes up on FRED and KEITH in topcoats, carrying cases. KEITH looks up to check train times.*)

FRED: So. Miss Cresswell won her case.

KEITH: She wouldn't have. If I hadn't summed up moderately in her favour.

FRED: Moderately?

KEITH: If I hadn't...well, done my best for her. Would you ever have told that story?

(*Long pause. FRED looks at him.*)

FRED: You think I wouldn't because I'm allergic to punishment?

KEITH: Something like that. Would you have brought yourself to pot me?

FRED: It'd be terrible for you, Keith, if you thought I wouldn't. I mean, you'd have given away all that mercy for nothing. All that effort to presume innocence. Entirely wasted.

KEITH: Well...?

FRED: So I'd better say that I would have told on you if you hadn't saved Byron. There now. Is that a more comfortable belief for you? Is that a kinder verdict?

KEITH: (*Angry.*) I don't need your bloody kindness!

FRED: Oh yes, you do, Keith. Everybody does.

(*They walk off together.*)

The End.